Monet

2005 TASCHEN DIARY
www.taschen.com

09–12.2004

SEPTEMBER	OCTOBER	NOVEMBER	DECEMBER
1 We	1 Fr	**WEEK 45**	1 We
2 Th	2 Sa	1 Mo	2 Th
3 Fr	3 Su	2 Tu	3 Fr
4 Sa	**WEEK 41**	3 We	4 Sa
5 Su	4 Mo	4 Th	5 Su ☽
WEEK 37	5 Tu	5 Fr ☽	**WEEK 50**
6 Mo ☽	6 We ☽	6 Sa	6 Mo
7 Tu	7 Th	7 Su	7 Tu
8 We	8 Fr	**WEEK 46**	8 We
9 Th	9 Sa	8 Mo	9 Th
10 Fr	10 Su	9 Tu	10 Fr
11 Sa	**WEEK 42**	10 We	11 Sa
12 Su	11 Mo	11 Th	12 Su ●
WEEK 38	12 Tu	12 Fr ●	**WEEK 51**
13 Mo	13 We	13 Sa	13 Mo
14 Tu ●	14 Th ●	14 Su	14 Tu
15 We	15 Fr	**WEEK 47**	15 We
16 Th	16 Sa	15 Mo	16 Th
17 Fr	17 Su	16 Tu	17 Fr
18 Sa	**WEEK 43**	17 We	18 Sa ◑
19 Su	18 Mo	18 Th	19 Su
WEEK 39	19 Tu	19 Fr ◑	**WEEK 52**
20 Mo	20 We ◑	20 Sa	20 Mo
21 Tu ◑	21 Th	21 Su	21 Tu
22 We	22 Fr	**WEEK 48**	22 We
23 Th	23 Sa	22 Mo	23 Th
24 Fr	24 Su	23 Tu	24 Fr
25 Sa	**WEEK 44**	24 We	25 Sa
26 Su	25 Mo	25 Th	26 Su ○
WEEK 40	26 Tu	26 Fr ○	**WEEK 53**
27 Mo	27 We	27 Sa	27 Mo
28 Tu ○	28 Th ○	28 Su	28 Tu
29 We	29 Fr	**WEEK 49**	29 We
30 Th	30 Sa	29 Mo	30 Th
	31 Su	30 Tu	31 Fr

01–04.2005

JANUARY	FEBRUARY	MARCH	APRIL
1 Sa	1 Tu	1 Tu	1 Fr
2 Su	2 We ☽	2 We	2 Sa ☽
WEEK 1	3 Th	3 Th ☽	3 Su
3 Mo ☽	4 Fr	4 Fr	**WEEK 14**
4 Tu	5 Sa	5 Sa	4 Mo
5 We	6 Su	6 Su	5 Tu
6 Th	**WEEK 6**	**WEEK 10**	6 We
7 Fr	7 Mo	7 Mo	7 Th
8 Sa	8 Tu ●	8 Tu	8 Fr ●
9 Su	9 We	9 We	9 Sa
WEEK 2	10 Th	10 Th ●	10 Su
10 Mo ●	11 Fr	11 Fr	**WEEK 15**
11 Tu	12 Sa	12 Sa	11 Mo
12 We	13 Su	13 Su	12 Tu
13 Th	**WEEK 7**	**WEEK 11**	13 We
14 Fr	14 Mo	14 Mo	14 Th
15 Sa	15 Tu	15 Tu	15 Fr
16 Su	16 We ◖	16 We	16 Sa ◖
WEEK 3	17 Th	17 Th ◖	17 Su
17 Mo ◖	18 Fr	18 Fr	**WEEK 16**
18 Tu	19 Sa	19 Sa	18 Mo
19 We	20 Su	20 Su	19 Tu
20 Th	**WEEK 8**	**WEEK 12**	20 We
21 Fr	21 Mo	21 Mo	21 Th
22 Sa	22 Tu	22 Tu	22 Fr
23 Su	23 We	23 We	23 Sa
WEEK 4	24 Th ○	24 Th	24 Su ○
24 Mo	25 Fr	25 Fr ○	**WEEK 17**
25 Tu ○	26 Sa	26 Sa	25 Mo
26 We	27 Su	27 Su	26 Tu
27 Th	**WEEK 9**	**WEEK 13**	27 We
28 Fr	28 Mo	28 Mo	28 Th
29 Sa		29 Tu	29 Fr
30 Su		30 We	30 Sa
WEEK 5		31 Th	
31 Mo			

05–08.2005

MAY

1 Su ◗

WEEK 18

2 Mo
3 Tu
4 We
5 Th
6 Fr
7 Sa
8 Su ●

WEEK 19

9 Mo
10 Tu
11 We
12 Th
13 Fr
14 Sa
15 Su

WEEK 20

16 Mo ◖
17 Tu
18 We
19 Th
20 Fr
21 Sa
22 Su

WEEK 21

23 Mo ○
24 Tu
25 We
26 Th
27 Fr
28 Sa
29 Su

WEEK 22

30 Mo ◗
31 Tu

JUNE

1 We
2 Th
3 Fr
4 Sa
5 Su

WEEK 23

6 Mo ●
7 Tu
8 We
9 Th
10 Fr
11 Sa
12 Su

WEEK 24

13 Mo
14 Tu
15 We ◖
16 Th
17 Fr
18 Sa
19 Su

WEEK 25

20 Mo
21 Tu
22 We ○
23 Th
24 Fr
25 Sa
26 Su

WEEK 26

27 Mo
28 Tu ◗
29 We
30 Th

JULY

1 Fr
2 Sa
3 Su

WEEK 27

4 Mo
5 Tu
6 We ●
7 Th
8 Fr
9 Sa
10 Su

WEEK 28

11 Mo
12 Tu
13 We
14 Th ◖
15 Fr
16 Sa
17 Su

WEEK 29

18 Mo
19 Tu
20 We
21 Th ○
22 Fr
23 Sa
24 Su

WEEK 30

25 Mo
26 Tu
27 We
28 Th ◗
29 Fr
30 Sa
31 Su

AUGUST

WEEK 31

1 Mo
2 Tu
3 We
4 Th
5 Fr ●
6 Sa
7 Su

WEEK 32

8 Mo
9 Tu
10 We
11 Th
12 Fr
13 Sa ◖
14 Su

WEEK 33

15 Mo
16 Tu
17 We
18 Th
19 Fr ○
20 Sa
21 Su

WEEK 34

22 Mo
23 Tu
24 We
25 Th
26 Fr ◗
27 Sa
28 Su

WEEK 35

29 Mo
30 Tu
31 We

09–12.2005

SEPTEMBER	OCTOBER	NOVEMBER	DECEMBER
1 Th	1 Sa	1 Tu	1 Th ●
2 Fr	2 Su	2 We ●	2 Fr
3 Sa ●	**WEEK 40**	3 Th	3 Sa
4 Su	3 Mo ●	4 Fr	4 Su
WEEK 36	4 Tu	5 Sa	**WEEK 49**
5 Mo	5 We	6 Su	5 Mo
6 Tu	6 Th	**WEEK 45**	6 Tu
7 We	7 Fr	7 Mo	7 We
8 Th	8 Sa	8 Tu	8 Th ◐
9 Fr	9 Su	9 We ◐	9 Fr
10 Sa	**WEEK 41**	10 Th	10 Sa
11 Su ◐	10 Mo ◐	11 Fr	11 Su
WEEK 37	11 Tu	12 Sa	**WEEK 50**
12 Mo	12 We	13 Su	12 Mo
13 Tu	13 Th	**WEEK 46**	13 Tu
14 We	14 Fr	14 Mo	14 We
15 Th	15 Sa	15 Tu	15 Th ○
16 Fr	16 Su	16 We ○	16 Fr
17 Sa	**WEEK 42**	17 Th	17 Sa
18 Su ○	17 Mo ○	18 Fr	18 Su
WEEK 38	18 Tu	19 Sa	**WEEK 51**
19 Mo	19 We	20 Su	19 Mo
20 Tu	20 Th	**WEEK 47**	20 Tu
21 We	21 Fr	21 Mo	21 We
22 Th	22 Sa	22 Tu	22 Th
23 Fr	23 Su	23 We ◑	23 Fr ◑
24 Sa	**WEEK 43**	24 Th	24 Sa
25 Su ◑	24 Mo	25 Fr	25 Su
WEEK 39	25 Tu ◑	26 Sa	**WEEK 52**
26 Mo	26 We	27 Su	26 Mo
27 Tu	27 Th	**WEEK 48**	27 Tu
28 We	28 Fr	28 Mo	28 We
29 Th	29 Sa	29 Tu	29 Th
30 Fr	30 Su	30 We	30 Fr
	WEEK 44		31 Sa ●
	31 Mo		

Portrait of Michel Wearing a Hat with a Pompom
1880. Oil on canvas, 46 x 38 cm
Paris, Musée Marmottan
Photo: Artothek, Weilheim / Peter Willi

Previous page: **Grainstacks at Sunset, Snow Effect** (detail)
1891. Oil on canvas, 65 x 100 cm
Chicago (IL), The Art Institute of Chicago

53. WEEK

12.2004 | 01.2005

Monday	27	3	10	17	24
Tuesday	28	4	11	18	25
Wednesday	29	5	12	19	26
Thursday	30	6	13	20	27
Friday	31	7	14	21	28
Saturday	1	8	15	22	29
Sunday	2	9	16	23	30
WEEK	53	1	2	3	4

Monday Montag Lundi Lunes Lunedì Segunda-feira Maandag 月

27

Tuesday Dienstag Mardi Martes Martedì Terça-feira Dinsdag 火

28

Wednesday Mittwoch Mercredi Miércoles Mercoledì Quarta-feira Woensdag 水

29

Thursday Donnerstag Jeudi Jueves Giovedì Quinta-feira Donderdag 木

30

Friday Freitag Vendredi Viernes Venerdì Sexta-feira Vrijdag 金

31

Saturday Samstag Samedi Sábado Sabato Sábado Zaterdag 土

New Year's Day | Jour de l'An |
Nouvel An | Neujahr | Capodanno |
Nieuwjaarsdag | Año Nuevo | Ano Novo

1

Sunday Sonntag Dimanche Domingo Domenica Domingo Zondag 日

2

1. WEEK

01.2005

Monday	3	10	17	24	31
Tuesday	4	11	18	25	1
Wednesday	5	12	19	26	2
Thursday	6	13	20	27	3
Friday	7	14	21	28	4
Saturday	8	15	22	29	5
Sunday	9	16	23	30	6
WEEK	1	2	3	4	5

Monday Montag Lundi Lunes Lunedì Segunda-feira Maandag 月

(UK) (CDN)
Public Holiday | Jour Férié

3

Tuesday Dienstag Mardi Martes Martedì Terça-feira Dinsdag 火

(UK) Public Holiday (Scotland only)

4

Wednesday Mittwoch Mercredi Miércoles Mercoledì Quarta-feira Woensdag 水

5

Thursday Donnerstag Jeudi Jueves Giovedì Quinta-feira Donderdag 木

(D) Heilige Drei Könige (teilweise)
(A) (E) (I) Heilige Drei Könige |
Reyes | Epifania

6

Friday Freitag Vendredi Viernes Venerdì Sexta-feira Vrijdag 金

7

Saturday Samstag Samedi Sábado Sabato Sábado Zaterdag 土

8

Sunday Sonntag Dimanche Domingo Domenica Domingo Zondag 日

9

Mount Kolsaas (detail)
1895. Oil on canvas, 65 x 100 cm
Private collection, United States

Previous page: **Apartement Interior**
1875. Oil on canvas, 80 x 60 cm
Paris, Musée d'Orsay
Photo: Artothek, Weilheim / Peter Willi

2. WEEK

01.2005

Monday	10	17	24	31	7
Tuesday	11	18	25	1	8
Wednesday	12	19	26	2	9
Thursday	13	20	27	3	10
Friday	14	21	28	4	11
Saturday	15	22	29	5	12
Sunday	16	23	30	6	13
WEEK	2	3	4	5	6

Monday Montag Lundi Lunes Lunedì Segunda-feira Maandag 月

●   Ⓙ Coming-of-Age Day

10

Tuesday Dienstag Mardi Martes Martedì Terça-feira Dinsdag 火

11

Wednesday Mittwoch Mercredi Miércoles Mercoledì Quarta-feira Woensdag 水

12

Thursday Donnerstag Jeudi Jueves Giovedì Quinta-feira Donderdag 木

13

Friday Freitag Vendredi Viernes Venerdì Sexta-feira Vrijdag 金

14

Saturday Samstag Samedi Sábado Sabato Sábado Zaterdag 土

15

Sunday Sonntag Dimanche Domingo Domenica Domingo Zondag 日

16

3. WEEK

01.2005

Monday	17	24	31	7	14
Tuesday	18	25	1	8	15
Wednesday	19	26	2	9	16
Thursday	20	27	3	10	17
Friday	21	28	4	11	18
Saturday	22	29	5	12	19
Sunday	23	30	6	13	20
WEEK	3	4	5	6	7

Monday Montag Lundi Lunes Lunedì Segunda-feira Maandag 月

◖   (USA) Martin Luther King Day

17

Tuesday Dienstag Mardi Martes Martedì Terça-feira Dinsdag 火

18

Wednesday Mittwoch Mercredi Miércoles Mercoledì Quarta-feira Woensdag 水

19

Thursday Donnerstag Jeudi Jueves Giovedì Quinta-feira Donderdag 木

20

Friday Freitag Vendredi Viernes Venerdì Sexta-feira Vrijdag 金

21

Saturday Samstag Samedi Sábado Sabato Sábado Zaterdag 土

22

Sunday Sonntag Dimanche Domingo Domenica Domingo Zondag 日

23

Camille with a Small Dog
1866. Oil on canvas, 73 x 54 cm
Zurich, Stiftung Sammlung Bührle
Photo: Artothek, Weilheim

Vétheuil
1901. Oil on canvas, 89 x 92 cm
Moscow, Pushkin Museum
Photo: Artothek, Weilheim

4. WEEK

01.2005

Monday	24	31	7	14	21
Tuesday	25	1	8	15	22
Wednesday	26	2	9	16	23
Thursday	27	3	10	17	24
Friday	28	4	11	18	25
Saturday	29	5	12	19	26
Sunday	30	6	13	20	27
WEEK	4	5	6	7	8

Monday Montag Lundi Lunes Lunedì Segunda-feira Maandag 月

24

Tuesday Dienstag Mardi Martes Martedì Terça-feira Dinsdag 火

○   (IL) Tu B'Shevat

25

Wednesday Mittwoch Mercredi Miércoles Mercoledì Quarta-feira Woensdag 水

26

Thursday Donnerstag Jeudi Jueves Giovedì Quinta-feira Donderdag 木

27

Friday Freitag Vendredi Viernes Venerdì Sexta-feira Vrijdag 金

28

Saturday Samstag Samedi Sábado Sabato Sábado Zaterdag 土

29

Sunday Sonntag Dimanche Domingo Domenica Domingo Zondag 日

30

5. ■ WEEK

01|02.2005

Monday	31	7	14	21	28
Tuesday	1	8	15	22	1
Wednesday	2	9	16	23	2
Thursday	3	10	17	24	3
Friday	4	11	18	25	4
Saturday	5	12	19	26	5
Sunday	6	13	20	27	6
WEEK	**5**	**6**	**7**	**8**	**9**

Monday Montag Lundi Lunes Lunedì Segunda-feira Maandag 月

31

Tuesday Dienstag Mardi Martes Martedì Terça-feira Dinsdag 火

1

Wednesday Mittwoch Mercredi Miércoles Mercoledì Quarta-feira Woensdag 水

2

Thursday Donnerstag Jeudi Jueves Giovedì Quinta-feira Donderdag 木

3

Friday Freitag Vendredi Viernes Venerdì Sexta-feira Vrijdag 金

4

Saturday Samstag Samedi Sábado Sabato Sábado Zaterdag 土

5

Sunday Sonntag Dimanche Domingo Domenica Domingo Zondag 日

6

The Red Kerchief, Portrait of Mrs. Monet
1873. Oil on canvas, 100 x 80 cm
Cleveland (OH), The Cleveland Museum of Art

Previous page:
Houses of Parliament, Sunset (detail)
1900–1901. Oil on canvas, 81 x 92 cm
Zurich, Kunsthaus Zürich

6. ■ WEEK

02.2005

Monday	7	14	21	28	7
Tuesday	8	15	22	1	8
Wednesday	9	16	23	2	9
Thursday	10	17	24	3	10
Friday	11	18	25	4	11
Saturday	12	19	26	5	12
Sunday	13	20	27	6	13
WEEK	**6**	**7**	**8**	**9**	**10**

Monday Montag Lundi Lunes Lunedì Segunda-feira Maandag 月

7

Tuesday Dienstag Mardi Martes Martedì Terça-feira Dinsdag 火

●

8

Wednesday Mittwoch Mercredi Miércoles Mercoledì Quarta-feira Woensdag 水

9

Thursday Donnerstag Jeudi Jueves Giovedì Quinta-feira Donderdag 木

10

Friday Freitag Vendredi Viernes Venerdì Sexta-feira Vrijdag 金

(J) Commemoration of the Founding
of the Nation

11

Saturday Samstag Samedi Sábado Sabato Sábado Zaterdag 土

12

Sunday Sonntag Dimanche Domingo Domenica Domingo Zondag 日

13

7. ■ WEEK

02.2005

Monday	14	21	28	7	14
Tuesday	15	22	1	8	15
Wednesday	16	23	2	9	16
Thursday	17	24	3	10	17
Friday	18	25	4	11	18
Saturday	19	26	5	12	19
Sunday	20	27	6	13	20
WEEK	7	8	9	10	11

Monday Montag Lundi Lunes Lunedì Segunda-feira Maandag 月

14

Tuesday Dienstag Mardi Martes Martedì Terça-feira Dinsdag 火

15

Wednesday Mittwoch Mercredi Miércoles Mercoledì Quarta-feira Woensdag 水

◖

16

Thursday Donnerstag Jeudi Jueves Giovedì Quinta-feira Donderdag 木

17

Friday Freitag Vendredi Viernes Venerdì Sexta-feira Vrijdag 金

18

Saturday Samstag Samedi Sábado Sabato Sábado Zaterdag 土

19

Sunday Sonntag Dimanche Domingo Domenica Domingo Zondag 日

20

Suzanne
1869–99. Pastel on canvas, 74 x 92 cm
New York, Christie's
Photo: Artothek, Weilheim / Christie's Images

The Portal (Grey Weather)
1892. Oil on canvas, 100 x 65 cm
Paris, Musée d'Orsay

8. ■ WEEK

02.2005

Monday	21	28	7	14	21
Tuesday	22	1	8	15	22
Wednesday	23	2	9	16	23
Thursday	24	3	10	17	24
Friday	25	4	11	18	25
Saturday	26	5	12	19	26
Sunday	27	6	13	20	27
WEEK	8	9	10	11	12

Monday Montag Lundi Lunes Lunedì Segunda-feira Maandag 月

(USA) President's Day

21

Tuesday Dienstag Mardi Martes Martedì Terça-feira Dinsdag 火

22

Wednesday Mittwoch Mercredi Miércoles Mercoledì Quarta-feira Woensdag 水

23

Thursday Donnerstag Jeudi Jueves Giovedì Quinta-feira Donderdag 木
○

24

Friday Freitag Vendredi Viernes Venerdì Sexta-feira Vrijdag 金

25

Saturday Samstag Samedi Sábado Sabato Sábado Zaterdag 土

26

Sunday Sonntag Dimanche Domingo Domenica Domingo Zondag 日

27

9. ■ WEEK

02|03.2005

Monday	28	7	14	21	28
Tuesday	1	8	15	22	29
Wednesday	2	9	16	23	30
Thursday	3	10	17	24	31
Friday	4	11	18	25	1
Saturday	5	12	19	26	2
Sunday	6	13	20	27	3
WEEK	9	10	11	12	13

Monday Montag Lundi Lunes Lunedì Segunda-feira Maandag 月

28

Tuesday Dienstag Mardi Martes Martedì Terça-feira Dinsdag 火

(ROK) Independence Movement Day

1

Wednesday Mittwoch Mercredi Miércoles Mercoledì Quarta-feira Woensdag 水

2

Thursday Donnerstag Jeudi Jueves Giovedì Quinta-feira Donderdag 木

◗

3

Friday Freitag Vendredi Viernes Venerdì Sexta-feira Vrijdag 金

4

Saturday Samstag Samedi Sábado Sabato Sábado Zaterdag 土

5

Sunday Sonntag Dimanche Domingo Domenica Domingo Zondag 日

6

Water-Lilies
1914–1917. Oil on canvas, 130 x 150 cm
Paris, Musée Marmottan

Previous page:
Impression, Sunrise
1873. Oil on canvas, 48 x 63 cm
Paris, Musée Marmottan

10. WEEK

03.2005

Monday	7	14	21	28	4
Tuesday	8	15	22	29	5
Wednesday	9	16	23	30	6
Thursday	10	17	24	31	7
Friday	11	18	25	1	8
Saturday	12	19	26	2	9
Sunday	13	20	27	3	10
WEEK	10	11	12	13	14

Monday Montag Lundi Lunes Lunedì Segunda-feira Maandag 月

7

Tuesday Dienstag Mardi Martes Martedì Terça-feira Dinsdag 火

8

Wednesday Mittwoch Mercredi Miércoles Mercoledì Quarta-feira Woensdag 水

9

Thursday Donnerstag Jeudi Jueves Giovedì Quinta-feira Donderdag 木
●

10

Friday Freitag Vendredi Viernes Venerdì Sexta-feira Vrijdag 金

11

Saturday Samstag Samedi Sábado Sabato Sábado Zaterdag 土

12

Sunday Sonntag Dimanche Domingo Domenica Domingo Zondag 日

13

11. WEEK

03.2005

Monday	14	21	28	4	11
Tuesday	15	22	29	5	12
Wednesday	16	23	30	6	13
Thursday	17	24	31	7	14
Friday	18	25	1	8	15
Saturday	19	26	2	9	16
Sunday	20	27	3	10	17
WEEK	**11**	**12**	**13**	**14**	**15**

Monday Montag Lundi Lunes Lunedì Segunda-feira Maandag 月

14

Tuesday Dienstag Mardi Martes Martedì Terça-feira Dinsdag 火

15

Wednesday Mittwoch Mercredi Miércoles Mercoledì Quarta-feira Woensdag 水

16

Thursday Donnerstag Jeudi Jueves Giovedì Quinta-feira Donderdag 木

◐

17

(UK) Saint Patrick's Day
(Northern Ireland only)
(IRL) Saint Patrick's Day

Friday Freitag Vendredi Viernes Venerdì Sexta-feira Vrijdag 金

18

Saturday Samstag Samedi Sábado Sabato Sábado Zaterdag 土

19

Sunday Sonntag Dimanche Domingo Domenica Domingo Zondag 日

(J) Vernal Equinox Day

20

Women in the Garden
1866. Oil on canvas, 256 x 208 cm
Paris, Musée d'Orsay

Previous page:
Grainstack at Sunset (detail)
1890–1891. Oil on canvas, 73 x 92 cm
Boston (MA), Museum of Fine Arts

12. WEEK

03.2005

Monday	21	28	4	11	18
Tuesday	22	29	5	12	19
Wednesday	23	30	6	13	20
Thursday	24	31	7	14	21
Friday	25	1	8	15	22
Saturday	26	2	9	16	23
Sunday	27	3	10	17	24
WEEK	12	13	14	15	16

Monday Montag Lundi Lunes Lunedì Segunda-feira Maandag 月

(J) Public Holiday

21

Tuesday Dienstag Mardi Martes Martedì Terça-feira Dinsdag 火

22

Wednesday Mittwoch Mercredi Miércoles Mercoledì Quarta-feira Woensdag 水

23

Thursday Donnerstag Jeudi Jueves Giovedì Quinta-feira Donderdag 木

24

Friday Freitag Vendredi Viernes Venerdì Sexta-feira Vrijdag 金

○

(UK) (CDN) (D) (CH) (E) (P)
Good Friday | Vendredi Saint |
Karfreitag | Venerdì Santo |
Viernes Santo | Sexta-feira Santa
(IL) Purim

25

Saturday Samstag Samedi Sábado Sabato Sábado Zaterdag 土

26

Sunday Sonntag Dimanche Domingo Domenica Domingo Zondag 日

Easter Sunday | Pâques | Ostersonntag |
Pasqua | 1e Paasdag | Pascua |
Domingo de Páscoa

27

13. WEEK

03|04.2005

Monday	28	4	11	18	25
Tuesday	29	5	12	19	26
Wednesday	30	6	13	20	27
Thursday	31	7	14	21	28
Friday	1	8	15	22	29
Saturday	2	9	16	23	30
Sunday	3	10	17	24	1
WEEK	13	14	15	16	17

Monday Montag Lundi Lunes Lunedì Segunda-feira Maandag 月

(UK) Easter Monday (except Scotland)
(IRL) (CDN) (F) (D) (A) (CH) (NL) (I)
Easter Monday | Lundi de Pâques |
Ostermontag | Lunedì di Pasqua |
2e Paasdag | Lunedì dell'Angelo

28

Tuesday Dienstag Mardi Martes Martedì Terça-feira Dinsdag 火

29

Wednesday Mittwoch Mercredi Miércoles Mercoledì Quarta-feira Woensdag 水

30

Thursday Donnerstag Jeudi Jueves Giovedì Quinta-feira Donderdag 木

31

Friday Freitag Vendredi Viernes Venerdì Sexta-feira Vrijdag 金

1

Saturday Samstag Samedi Sábado Sabato Sábado Zaterdag 土

◐

2

Sunday Sonntag Dimanche Domingo Domenica Domingo Zondag 日

3

Study of a Figure Outdoors (Facing Right, detail)
1886. Oil on canvas, 131 x 88 cm
Paris, Musée d'Orsay

Previous page:
Camille and Jean Monet in the Garden at Argenteuil
1873. Oil on canvas, 131 x 97 cm
Private collection

14. WEEK

04.2005

Monday	4	11	18	25	2
Tuesday	5	12	19	26	3
Wednesday	6	13	20	27	4
Thursday	7	14	21	28	5
Friday	8	15	22	29	6
Saturday	9	16	23	30	7
Sunday	10	17	24	1	8
WEEK	**14**	**15**	**16**	**17**	**18**

Monday Montag Lundi Lunes Lunedì Segunda-feira Maandag 月

4

Tuesday Dienstag Mardi Martes Martedì Terça-feira Dinsdag 火

(ROK) Arbor Day

5

Wednesday Mittwoch Mercredi Miércoles Mercoledì Quarta-feira Woensdag 水

6

Thursday Donnerstag Jeudi Jueves Giovedì Quinta-feira Donderdag 木

7

Friday Freitag Vendredi Viernes Venerdì Sexta-feira Vrijdag 金

8

Saturday Samstag Samedi Sábado Sabato Sábado Zaterdag 土

9

Sunday Sonntag Dimanche Domingo Domenica Domingo Zondag 日

10

15. WEEK

04.2005

Monday	11	18	25	2	9
Tuesday	12	19	26	3	10
Wednesday	13	20	27	4	11
Thursday	14	21	28	5	12
Friday	15	22	29	6	13
Saturday	16	23	30	7	14
Sunday	17	24	1	8	15
WEEK	15	16	17	18	19

Monday Montag Lundi Lunes Lunedì Segunda-feira Maandag 月

11

Tuesday Dienstag Mardi Martes Martedì Terça-feira Dinsdag 火

12

Wednesday Mittwoch Mercredi Miércoles Mercoledì Quarta-feira Woensdag 水

13

Thursday Donnerstag Jeudi Jueves Giovedì Quinta-feira Donderdag 木

14

Friday Freitag Vendredi Viernes Venerdì Sexta-feira Vrijdag 金

15

Saturday Samstag Samedi Sábado Sabato Sábado Zaterdag 土

16

Sunday Sonntag Dimanche Domingo Domenica Domingo Zondag 日

17

Water-Lily Pond
1897–1899. Oil on canvas, 90 x 90 cm
Princeton (NJ), The Art Museum, Princeton University

Etretat: The Beach and the Porte d'Aval (detail)
1884. Oil on canvas, 60 x 73 cm
Tokyo, Murauchi Art Museum, Hachioji

16. WEEK

04.2005

Monday	18	25	2	9	16
Tuesday	19	26	3	10	17
Wednesday	20	27	4	11	18
Thursday	21	28	5	12	19
Friday	22	29	6	13	20
Saturday	23	30	7	14	21
Sunday	24	1	8	15	22
WEEK	**16**	**17**	**18**	**19**	**20**

Monday Montag Lundi Lunes Lunedì Segunda-feira Maandag 月

18

Tuesday Dienstag Mardi Martes Martedì Terça-feira Dinsdag 火

19

Wednesday Mittwoch Mercredi Miércoles Mercoledì Quarta-feira Woensdag 水

20

Thursday Donnerstag Jeudi Jueves Giovedì Quinta-feira Donderdag 木

21

Friday Freitag Vendredi Viernes Venerdì Sexta-feira Vrijdag 金

22

Saturday Samstag Samedi Sábado Sabato Sábado Zaterdag 土

23

Sunday Sonntag Dimanche Domingo Domenica Domingo Zondag 日

(IL) Passover

24

17. WEEK

04 | 05.2005

Monday	25	2	9	16	23
Tuesday	26	3	10	17	24
Wednesday	27	4	11	18	25
Thursday	28	5	12	19	26
Friday	29	6	13	20	27
Saturday	30	7	14	21	28
Sunday	1	8	15	22	29
WEEK	17	18	19	20	21

Monday Montag Lundi Lunes Lunedì Segunda-feira Maandag 月

Ⓘ Liberazione
Ⓟ Dia da Liberdade

25

Tuesday Dienstag Mardi Martes Martedì Terça-feira Dinsdag 火

26

Wednesday Mittwoch Mercredi Miércoles Mercoledì Quarta-feira Woensdag 水

27

Thursday Donnerstag Jeudi Jueves Giovedì Quinta-feira Donderdag 木

28

Friday Freitag Vendredi Viernes Venerdì Sexta-feira Vrijdag 金

Ⓙ Greenery Day

29

Saturday Samstag Samedi Sábado Sabato Sábado Zaterdag 土

Ⓝ Koninginnedag

30

Sunday Sonntag Dimanche Domingo Domenica Domingo Zondag 日

◑

Ⓕ Ⓓ Ⓐ Ⓘ Ⓟ
Fête du Travail | Maifeiertag |
Festa del Lavoro | Dia do Trabalhador
Ⓘⓛ Passover

1

The Path under the Rose Arches
1920–1922. Oil on canvas, 92 x 89 cm
Paris, Musée Marmottan
Photo: Artothek, Weilheim / Peter Willi

Following page:
The Bodmer Oak
1865. Oil on canvas, 54 x 40 cm
Private collection, United States

18. WEEK

05.2005

Monday	2	9	16	23	30
Tuesday	3	10	17	24	31
Wednesday	4	11	18	25	1
Thursday	5	12	19	26	2
Friday	6	13	20	27	3
Saturday	7	14	21	28	4
Sunday	8	15	22	29	5
WEEK	**18**	**19**	**20**	**21**	**22**

Monday Montag Lundi Lunes Lunedì Segunda-feira Maandag 月

(UK) (IRL)
Early May Bank Holiday
(E) Fiesta del Trabajo

2

Tuesday Dienstag Mardi Martes Martedì Terça-feira Dinsdag 火

(J) Constitution Day

3

Wednesday Mittwoch Mercredi Miércoles Mercoledì Quarta-feira Woensdag 水

(J) Public Holiday

4

Thursday Donnerstag Jeudi Jueves Giovedì Quinta-feira Donderdag 木

(F) (D) (A) (CH) (NL)
Ascension | Christi Himmelfahrt |
Auffahrt | Ascensione | Hemelvaartsdag
(J) (ROK) Children's Day
(IL) Yom Hashoah

5

Friday Freitag Vendredi Viernes Venerdì Sexta-feira Vrijdag 金

6

Saturday Samstag Samedi Sábado Sabato Sábado Zaterdag 土

7

Sunday Sonntag Dimanche Domingo Domenica Domingo Zondag 日

(F) Fête de la Libération

8

19. ■ WEEK

05.2005

Monday	9	16	23	30	6
Tuesday	10	17	24	31	7
Wednesday	11	18	25	1	8
Thursday	12	19	26	2	9
Friday	13	20	27	3	10
Saturday	14	21	28	4	11
Sunday	15	22	29	5	12
WEEK	19	20	21	22	23

Monday Montag Lundi Lunes Lunedì Segunda-feira Maandag 月

9

Tuesday Dienstag Mardi Martes Martedì Terça-feira Dinsdag 火

10

Wednesday Mittwoch Mercredi Miércoles Mercoledì Quarta-feira Woensdag 水

11

Thursday Donnerstag Jeudi Jueves Giovedì Quinta-feira Donderdag 木

(IL) Yom Haazmaut

12

Friday Freitag Vendredi Viernes Venerdì Sexta-feira Vrijdag 金

13

Saturday Samstag Samedi Sábado Sabato Sábado Zaterdag 土

14

Sunday Sonntag Dimanche Domingo Domenica Domingo Zondag 日

(F) (D) (A) (CH) (NL)
Pentecôte | Pfingstsonntag |
Pentecoste | 1e Pinksterdag
(ROK) Buddha's Birthday

15

Luncheon on the Grass, Central Panel
1865. Oil on canvas, 248 x 217 cm
Paris, Musée d'Orsay

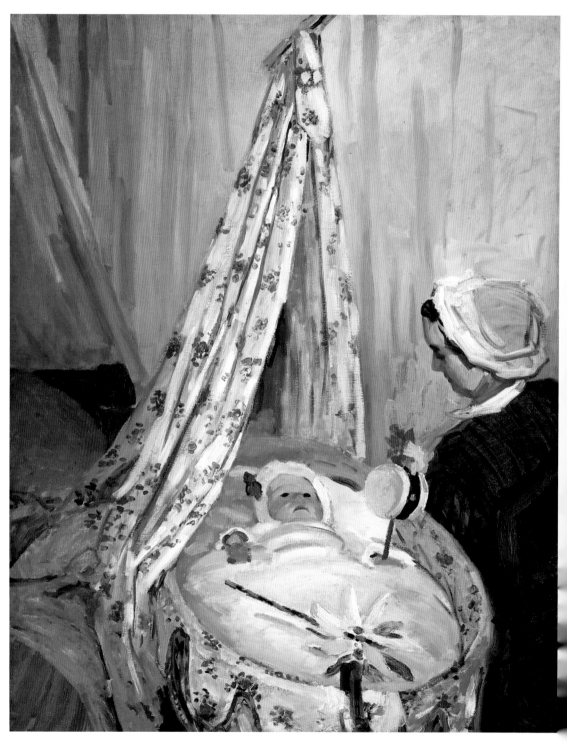

Jean Monet in his Cradle
1867. Oil on canvas, 116 x 89 cm
Washington, D.C., National Gallery of Art

20. ■ WEEK

05.2005

Monday	16	23	30	6	13
Tuesday	17	24	31	7	14
Wednesday	18	25	1	8	15
Thursday	19	26	2	9	16
Friday	20	27	3	10	17
Saturday	21	28	4	11	18
Sunday	22	29	5	12	19
WEEK	**20**	**21**	**22**	**23**	**24**

Monday Montag Lundi Lunes Lunedì Segunda-feira Maandag 月

◗

Ⓓ Ⓐ ⒸⒽ ⓃⓁ

Pfingstmontag | Lundi de Pentecôte |
Lunedì di Pentecoste | 2ᵉ Pinksterdag

16

Tuesday Dienstag Mardi Martes Martedì Terça-feira Dinsdag 火

17

Wednesday Mittwoch Mercredi Miércoles Mercoledì Quarta-feira Woensdag 水

18

Thursday Donnerstag Jeudi Jueves Giovedì Quinta-feira Donderdag 木

19

Friday Freitag Vendredi Viernes Venerdì Sexta-feira Vrijdag 金

20

Saturday Samstag Samedi Sábado Sabato Sábado Zaterdag 土

21

Sunday Sonntag Dimanche Domingo Domenica Domingo Zondag 日

22

---

21. ■ WEEK

05.2005

Monday	23	30	6	13	20
Tuesday	24	31	7	14	21
Wednesday	25	1	8	15	22
Thursday	26	2	9	16	23
Friday	27	3	10	17	24
Saturday	28	4	11	18	25
Sunday	29	5	12	19	26
WEEK	**21**	**22**	**23**	**24**	**25**

Monday Montag Lundi Lunes Lunedì Segunda-feira Maandag 月

○   (CDN) Victoria Day | Fête de la Reine

23

Tuesday Dienstag Mardi Martes Martedì Terça-feira Dinsdag 火

24

Wednesday Mittwoch Mercredi Miércoles Mercoledì Quarta-feira Woensdag 水

25

Thursday Donnerstag Jeudi Jueves Giovedì Quinta-feira Donderdag 木

(D) Fronleichnam (teilweise)
(A) Fronleichnam
(P) Corpo de Deus

26

Friday Freitag Vendredi Viernes Venerdì Sexta-feira Vrijdag 金

27

Saturday Samstag Samedi Sábado Sabato Sábado Zaterdag 土

28

Sunday Sonntag Dimanche Domingo Domenica Domingo Zondag 日

29

Camille Monet at the Window
1873. Oil on canvas, 60 x 49.5 cm
Richmond (VA), Virginia Museum of Fine Arts

Previous page:
Poppies at Argenteuil (detail)
1873. Oil on canvas, 50 x 65 cm
Paris, Musée d'Orsay

22. WEEK

05|06.2005

Monday	30	6	13	20	27
Tuesday	31	7	14	21	28
Wednesday	1	8	15	22	29
Thursday	2	9	16	23	30
Friday	3	10	17	24	1
Saturday	4	11	18	25	2
Sunday	5	12	19	26	3
WEEK	22	23	24	25	26

Monday Montag Lundi Lunes Lunedì Segunda-feira Maandag 月

☽   (USA) Memorial Day
                                                     (UK) Spring Bank Holiday

30

Tuesday Dienstag Mardi Martes Martedì Terça-feira Dinsdag 火

31

Wednesday Mittwoch Mercredi Miércoles Mercoledì Quarta-feira Woensdag 水

1

Thursday Donnerstag Jeudi Jueves Giovedì Quinta-feira Donderdag 木

                                                     (I) Festa della Repubblica

2

Friday Freitag Vendredi Viernes Venerdì Sexta-feira Vrijdag 金

3

Saturday Samstag Samedi Sábado Sabato Sábado Zaterdag 土

4

Sunday Sonntag Dimanche Domingo Domenica Domingo Zondag 日

5

23. WEEK

06.2005

Monday	6	13	20	27	4
Tuesday	7	14	21	28	5
Wednesday	8	15	22	29	6
Thursday	9	16	23	30	7
Friday	10	17	24	1	8
Saturday	11	18	25	2	9
Sunday	12	19	26	3	10
WEEK	**23**	**24**	**25**	**26**	**27**

Monday Montag Lundi Lunes Lunedì Segunda-feira Maandag 月

●

(IRL) First Monday in June
(ROK) Memorial Day

6

Tuesday Dienstag Mardi Martes Martedì Terça-feira Dinsdag 火

7

Wednesday Mittwoch Mercredi Miércoles Mercoledì Quarta-feira Woensdag 水

8

Thursday Donnerstag Jeudi Jueves Giovedì Quinta-feira Donderdag 木

9

Friday Freitag Vendredi Viernes Venerdì Sexta-feira Vrijdag 金

(P) Dia Nacional

10

Saturday Samstag Samedi Sábado Sabato Sábado Zaterdag 土

11

Sunday Sonntag Dimanche Domingo Domenica Domingo Zondag 日

12

Hôtel des Roches Noires, Trouville
1870. Oil on canvas, 80 x 55 cm
Paris, Musée d'Orsay

Suzanne Reading and Blanche Painting by the Marsh at Giverny
1887. Oil on canvas, 91.5 x 98 cm
Los Angeles (CA), Los Angeles County Museum of Art

24. WEEK

06.2005

Monday	13	20	27	4	11
Tuesday	14	21	28	5	12
Wednesday	15	22	29	6	13
Thursday	16	23	30	7	14
Friday	17	24	1	8	15
Saturday	18	25	2	9	16
Sunday	19	26	3	10	17
WEEK	24	25	26	27	28

Monday Montag Lundi Lunes Lunedì Segunda-feira Maandag 月

(IL) Shavuot

13

Tuesday Dienstag Mardi Martes Martedì Terça-feira Dinsdag 火

14

Wednesday Mittwoch Mercredi Miércoles Mercoledì Quarta-feira Woensdag 水

◖

15

Thursday Donnerstag Jeudi Jueves Giovedì Quinta-feira Donderdag 木

16

Friday Freitag Vendredi Viernes Venerdì Sexta-feira Vrijdag 金

17

Saturday Samstag Samedi Sábado Sabato Sábado Zaterdag 土

18

Sunday Sonntag Dimanche Domingo Domenica Domingo Zondag 日

19

25. ■ WEEK

06.2005

Monday	20	27	4	11	18
Tuesday	21	28	5	12	19
Wednesday	22	29	6	13	20
Thursday	23	30	7	14	21
Friday	24	1	8	15	22
Saturday	25	2	9	16	23
Sunday	26	3	10	17	24
WEEK	25	26	27	28	29

Monday Montag Lundi Lunes Lunedì Segunda-feira Maandag 月

20

Tuesday Dienstag Mardi Martes Martedì Terça-feira Dinsdag 火

21

Wednesday Mittwoch Mercredi Miércoles Mercoledì Quarta-feira Woensdag 水
○

22

Thursday Donnerstag Jeudi Jueves Giovedì Quinta-feira Donderdag 木

23

Friday Freitag Vendredi Viernes Venerdì Sexta-feira Vrijdag 金

24

Saturday Samstag Samedi Sábado Sabato Sábado Zaterdag 土

25

Sunday Sonntag Dimanche Domingo Domenica Domingo Zondag 日

26

Villas at Bordighera (detail)
1884. Oil on canvas, 73 x 92 cm
Santa Barbara (CA), Santa Barbara Museum of Art

Poplars, White and Yellow Effect
1891. Oil on canvas, 100 x 65 cm
Philadelphia (PA), Philadelphia Museum of Art

26. WEEK

06 | 07.2005

Monday	27	4	11	18	25
Tuesday	28	5	12	19	26
Wednesday	29	6	13	20	27
Thursday	30	7	14	21	28
Friday	1	8	15	22	29
Saturday	2	9	16	23	30
Sunday	3	10	17	24	31
WEEK	26	27	28	29	30

Monday Montag Lundi Lunes Lunedì Segunda-feira Maandag 月

27

Tuesday Dienstag Mardi Martes Martedì Terça-feira Dinsdag 火

28

Wednesday Mittwoch Mercredi Miércoles Mercoledì Quarta-feira Woensdag 水

29

Thursday Donnerstag Jeudi Jueves Giovedì Quinta-feira Donderdag 木

30

Friday Freitag Vendredi Viernes Venerdì Sexta-feira Vrijdag 金

CDN Canada Day | Fête du Canada

1

Saturday Samstag Samedi Sábado Sabato Sábado Zaterdag 土

2

Sunday Sonntag Dimanche Domingo Domenica Domingo Zondag 日

3

27. ■ WEEK

07.2005

Monday	4	11	18	25	1
Tuesday	5	12	19	26	2
Wednesday	6	13	20	27	3
Thursday	7	14	21	28	4
Friday	8	15	22	29	5
Saturday	9	16	23	30	6
Sunday	10	17	24	31	7
WEEK	27	28	29	30	31

Monday Montag Lundi Lunes Lunedì Segunda-feira Maandag 月

(USA) Independence Day

4

Tuesday Dienstag Mardi Martes Martedì Terça-feira Dinsdag 火

5

Wednesday Mittwoch Mercredi Miércoles Mercoledì Quarta-feira Woensdag 水

●

6

Thursday Donnerstag Jeudi Jueves Giovedì Quinta-feira Donderdag 木

7

Friday Freitag Vendredi Viernes Venerdì Sexta-feira Vrijdag 金

8

Saturday Samstag Samedi Sábado Sabato Sábado Zaterdag 土

9

Sunday Sonntag Dimanche Domingo Domenica Domingo Zondag 日

10

Monet's Garden at Vétheuil
1881. Oil on canvas, 150 x 120 cm
Washington, D.C., National Gallery of Art

Previous page: **Woman Sitting on a Bench**
1878. Oil on canvas, 74 x 56 cm
London, Tate Gallery
Photo: Artothek, Weilheim / G. Westermann

28. ■ WEEK

07.2005

Monday	11	18	25	1	8
Tuesday	12	19	26	2	9
Wednesday	13	20	27	3	10
Thursday	14	21	28	4	11
Friday	15	22	29	5	12
Saturday	16	23	30	6	13
Sunday	17	24	31	7	14
WEEK	28	29	30	31	32

Monday Montag Lundi Lunes Lunedì Segunda-feira Maandag 月

11

Tuesday Dienstag Mardi Martes Martedì Terça-feira Dinsdag 火

(UK) Battle of the Boyne Day
(Northern Ireland only)

12

Wednesday Mittwoch Mercredi Miércoles Mercoledì Quarta-feira Woensdag 水

13

Thursday Donnerstag Jeudi Jueves Giovedì Quinta-feira Donderdag 木

(F) Fête Nationale

14

Friday Freitag Vendredi Viernes Venerdì Sexta-feira Vrijdag 金

15

Saturday Samstag Samedi Sábado Sabato Sábado Zaterdag 土

16

Sunday Sonntag Dimanche Domingo Domenica Domingo Zondag 日

(ROK) Constitution Day

17

29. ■WEEK

07.2005

Monday	18	25	1	8	15
Tuesday	19	26	2	9	16
Wednesday	20	27	3	10	17
Thursday	21	28	4	11	18
Friday	22	29	5	12	19
Saturday	23	30	6	13	20
Sunday	24	31	7	14	21
WEEK	29	30	31	32	33

Monday Montag Lundi Lunes Lunedì Segunda-feira Maandag 月

Ⓙ Marine Day

18

Tuesday Dienstag Mardi Martes Martedì Terça-feira Dinsdag 火

19

Wednesday Mittwoch Mercredi Miércoles Mercoledì Quarta-feira Woensdag 水

20

Thursday Donnerstag Jeudi Jueves Giovedì Quinta-feira Donderdag 木

○

21

Friday Freitag Vendredi Viernes Venerdì Sexta-feira Vrijdag 金

22

Saturday Samstag Samedi Sábado Sabato Sábado Zaterdag 土

23

Sunday Sonntag Dimanche Domingo Domenica Domingo Zondag 日

24

Entrance to the Port of Trouville
1870. Oil on canvas, 54 x 66 cm
Budapest, Szépművészeti Múzeum

The Walk, Woman with a Parasol
1875. Oil on canvas, 100 x 81 cm
Washington, D.C., National Gallery of Art

30. WEEK

07.2005

Monday	25	1	8	15	22
Tuesday	26	2	9	16	23
Wednesday	27	3	10	17	24
Thursday	28	4	11	18	25
Friday	29	5	12	19	26
Saturday	30	6	13	20	27
Sunday	31	7	14	21	28
WEEK	**30**	**31**	**32**	**33**	**34**

Monday Montag Lundi Lunes Lunedì Segunda-feira Maandag 月

25

Tuesday Dienstag Mardi Martes Martedì Terça-feira Dinsdag 火

26

Wednesday Mittwoch Mercredi Miércoles Mercoledì Quarta-feira Woensdag 水

27

Thursday Donnerstag Jeudi Jueves Giovedì Quinta-feira Donderdag 木

28

Friday Freitag Vendredi Viernes Venerdì Sexta-feira Vrijdag 金

29

Saturday Samstag Samedi Sábado Sabato Sábado Zaterdag 土

30

Sunday Sonntag Dimanche Domingo Domenica Domingo Zondag 日

31

31. WEEK

08.2005

Monday	1	8	15	22	29
Tuesday	2	9	16	23	30
Wednesday	3	10	17	24	31
Thursday	4	11	18	25	1
Friday	5	12	19	26	2
Saturday	6	13	20	27	3
Sunday	7	14	21	28	4
WEEK	**31**	**32**	**33**	**34**	**35**

Monday Montag Lundi Lunes Lunedì Segunda-feira Maandag 月

1

(UK) Summer Bank Holiday
(Scotland only)
(IRL) First Monday in August
(CH) Bundesfeiertag | Fête nationale |
Festa nazionale

Tuesday Dienstag Mardi Martes Martedì Terça-feira Dinsdag 火

2

Wednesday Mittwoch Mercredi Miércoles Mercoledì Quarta-feira Woensdag 水

3

Thursday Donnerstag Jeudi Jueves Giovedì Quinta-feira Donderdag 木

4

Friday Freitag Vendredi Viernes Venerdì Sexta-feira Vrijdag 金

●

5

Saturday Samstag Samedi Sábado Sabato Sábado Zaterdag 土

6

Sunday Sonntag Dimanche Domingo Domenica Domingo Zondag 日

7

Main Path through the Garden at Giverny
1902. Oil on canvas, 89 x 92 cm
Vienna, Österreichische Galerie
Photo: Artothek, Weilheim / Photobusiness

Water-Lilies and Agapanthus
1914–1917. Oil on canvas, 140 x 120 cm
Paris, Musée Marmottan

32. WEEK

08.2005

Monday	8	15	22	29	5
Tuesday	9	16	23	30	6
Wednesday	10	17	24	31	7
Thursday	11	18	25	1	8
Friday	12	19	26	2	9
Saturday	13	20	27	3	10
Sunday	14	21	28	4	11
WEEK	**32**	**33**	**34**	**35**	**36**

Monday Montag Lundi Lunes Lunedì Segunda-feira Maandag 月

8

Tuesday Dienstag Mardi Martes Martedì Terça-feira Dinsdag 火

9

Wednesday Mittwoch Mercredi Miércoles Mercoledì Quarta-feira Woensdag 水

10

Thursday Donnerstag Jeudi Jueves Giovedì Quinta-feira Donderdag 木

11

Friday Freitag Vendredi Viernes Venerdì Sexta-feira Vrijdag 金

12

Saturday Samstag Samedi Sábado Sabato Sábado Zaterdag 土

13

Sunday Sonntag Dimanche Domingo Domenica Domingo Zondag 日

(IL) Tisha B'Av

14

33. WEEK

08.2005

Monday	15	22	29	5	12
Tuesday	16	23	30	6	13
Wednesday	17	24	31	7	14
Thursday	18	25	1	8	15
Friday	19	26	2	9	16
Saturday	20	27	3	10	17
Sunday	21	28	4	11	18
WEEK	33	34	35	36	37

Monday Montag Lundi Lunes Lunedì Segunda-feira Maandag 月

15

(D) Mariä Himmelfahrt (teilweise)

(F) (A) (E) (I) (P)
Assomption | Mariä Himmelfahrt |
Asunción de la Virgen | Assunzione |
Assunção de Nossa Senhora
(ROK) Independence Day

Tuesday Dienstag Mardi Martes Martedì Terça-feira Dinsdag 火

16

Wednesday Mittwoch Mercredi Miércoles Mercoledì Quarta-feira Woensdag 水

17

Thursday Donnerstag Jeudi Jueves Giovedì Quinta-feira Donderdag 木

18

Friday Freitag Vendredi Viernes Venerdì Sexta-feira Vrijdag 金
○

19

Saturday Samstag Samedi Sábado Sabato Sábado Zaterdag 土

20

Sunday Sonntag Dimanche Domingo Domenica Domingo Zondag 日

21

Jar of Peaches
1866. Oil on canvas, 55.4 x 46 cm
Dresden, Gemäldegalerie
Photo: Artothek, Weilheim

Following page: **Path in the Forest**
1865. Oil on canvas, 79 x 58 cm
London, Christie's
Photo: Artothek, Weilheim / Christie's Images

34. WEEK

08.2005

Monday	22	29	5	12	19
Tuesday	23	30	6	13	20
Wednesday	24	31	7	14	21
Thursday	25	1	8	15	22
Friday	26	2	9	16	23
Saturday	27	3	10	17	24
Sunday	28	4	11	18	25
WEEK	34	35	36	37	38

Monday Montag Lundi Lunes Lunedì Segunda-feira Maandag 月

22

Tuesday Dienstag Mardi Martes Martedì Terça-feira Dinsdag 火

23

Wednesday Mittwoch Mercredi Miércoles Mercoledì Quarta-feira Woensdag 水

24

Thursday Donnerstag Jeudi Jueves Giovedì Quinta-feira Donderdag 木

25

Friday Freitag Vendredi Viernes Venerdì Sexta-feira Vrijdag 金

◗

26

Saturday Samstag Samedi Sábado Sabato Sábado Zaterdag 土

27

Sunday Sonntag Dimanche Domingo Domenica Domingo Zondag 日

28

35. WEEK

08|09.2005

Monday	29	5	12	19	26
Tuesday	30	6	13	20	27
Wednesday	31	7	14	21	28
Thursday	1	8	15	22	29
Friday	2	9	16	23	30
Saturday	3	10	17	24	1
Sunday	4	11	18	25	2
WEEK	**35**	**36**	**37**	**38**	**39**

Monday Montag Lundi Lunes Lunedì Segunda-feira Maandag 月

(UK) Summer Bank Holiday

(except Scotland)

29

Tuesday Dienstag Mardi Martes Martedì Terça-feira Dinsdag 火

30

Wednesday Mittwoch Mercredi Miércoles Mercoledì Quarta-feira Woensdag 水

31

Thursday Donnerstag Jeudi Jueves Giovedì Quinta-feira Donderdag 木

1

Friday Freitag Vendredi Viernes Venerdì Sexta-feira Vrijdag 金

2

Saturday Samstag Samedi Sábado Sabato Sábado Zaterdag 土

●

3

Sunday Sonntag Dimanche Domingo Domenica Domingo Zondag 日

4

Yellow Irises
1914–1917. Oil on canvas, 200 x 100 cm
New York, Christie's
Photo: Artothek, Weilheim / Christie's Images

Weeping Willow
1922. Oil on canvas, 110.5 x 100 cm
Basle, Galerie Beyeler
Photo: Artothek, Weilheim / Hans Hinz

36. WEEK

09.2005

Monday	5	12	19	26	3
Tuesday	6	13	20	27	4
Wednesday	7	14	21	28	5
Thursday	8	15	22	29	6
Friday	9	16	23	30	7
Saturday	10	17	24	1	8
Sunday	11	18	25	2	9
WEEK	36	37	38	39	40

Monday Montag Lundi Lunes Lunedì Segunda-feira Maandag 月

(USA) Labor Day
(CDN) Labour Day | Fête du Travail

5

Tuesday Dienstag Mardi Martes Martedì Terça-feira Dinsdag 火

6

Wednesday Mittwoch Mercredi Miércoles Mercoledì Quarta-feira Woensdag 水

7

Thursday Donnerstag Jeudi Jueves Giovedì Quinta-feira Donderdag 木

8

Friday Freitag Vendredi Viernes Venerdì Sexta-feira Vrijdag 金

9

Saturday Samstag Samedi Sábado Sabato Sábado Zaterdag 土

10

Sunday Sonntag Dimanche Domingo Domenica Domingo Zondag 日

11

---

37. ■ WEEK

09.2005

Monday	12	19	26	3	10
Tuesday	13	20	27	4	11
Wednesday	14	21	28	5	12
Thursday	15	22	29	6	13
Friday	16	23	30	7	14
Saturday	17	24	1	8	15
Sunday	18	25	2	9	16
WEEK	37	38	39	40	41

Monday Montag Lundi Lunes Lunedì Segunda-feira Maandag 月

12

Tuesday Dienstag Mardi Martes Martedì Terça-feira Dinsdag 火

13

Wednesday Mittwoch Mercredi Miércoles Mercoledì Quarta-feira Woensdag 水

14

Thursday Donnerstag Jeudi Jueves Giovedì Quinta-feira Donderdag 木

15

Friday Freitag Vendredi Viernes Venerdì Sexta-feira Vrijdag 金

16

Saturday Samstag Samedi Sábado Sabato Sábado Zaterdag 土

17

Sunday Sonntag Dimanche Domingo Domenica Domingo Zondag 日

○   (ROK) Chuseok

18

Landscape with Figures, Giverny
1888. Oil on canvas, 80 x 80 cm
Chicago (IL), The Art Institute of Chicago

Bouquet of Sunflowers
1880. Oil on canvas, 101 x 81.5 cm
New York (NY), The Metropolitan Museum of Art

38. WEEK

09.2005

Monday	19	26	3	10	17
Tuesday	20	27	4	11	18
Wednesday	21	28	5	12	19
Thursday	22	29	6	13	20
Friday	23	30	7	14	21
Saturday	24	1	8	15	22
Sunday	25	2	9	16	23
WEEK	**38**	**39**	**40**	**41**	**42**

Monday Montag Lundi Lunes Lunedì Segunda-feira Maandag 月

ⓙ Respect-for-the-Aged Day

19

Tuesday Dienstag Mardi Martes Martedì Terça-feira Dinsdag 火

20

Wednesday Mittwoch Mercredi Miércoles Mercoledì Quarta-feira Woensdag 水

21

Thursday Donnerstag Jeudi Jueves Giovedì Quinta-feira Donderdag 木

22

Friday Freitag Vendredi Viernes Venerdì Sexta-feira Vrijdag 金

ⓙ Autumn Equinox Day

23

Saturday Samstag Samedi Sábado Sabato Sábado Zaterdag 土

24

Sunday Sonntag Dimanche Domingo Domenica Domingo Zondag 日

25

39. ■ WEEK

09|10.2005

Monday	26	3	10	17	24
Tuesday	27	4	11	18	25
Wednesday	28	5	12	19	26
Thursday	29	6	13	20	27
Friday	30	7	14	21	28
Saturday	1	8	15	22	29
Sunday	2	9	16	23	30
WEEK	39	40	41	42	43

Monday Montag Lundi Lunes Lunedì Segunda-feira Maandag 月

26

Tuesday Dienstag Mardi Martes Martedì Terça-feira Dinsdag 火

27

Wednesday Mittwoch Mercredi Miércoles Mercoledì Quarta-feira Woensdag 水

28

Thursday Donnerstag Jeudi Jueves Giovedì Quinta-feira Donderdag 木

29

Friday Freitag Vendredi Viernes Venerdì Sexta-feira Vrijdag 金

30

Saturday Samstag Samedi Sábado Sabato Sábado Zaterdag 土

1

Sunday Sonntag Dimanche Domingo Domenica Domingo Zondag 日

2

Water-Lilies
1908. Oil on canvas, 100 x 100 cm
Private collection

Following page:
Rocks at Belle-Ile
1886. Oil on canvas, 60 x 73 cm
Copenhagen, Ny Carlsberg Glyptotek

40. WEEK

10.2005

Monday	3	10	17	24	31
Tuesday	4	11	18	25	1
Wednesday	5	12	19	26	2
Thursday	6	13	20	27	3
Friday	7	14	21	28	4
Saturday	8	15	22	29	5
Sunday	9	16	23	30	6
WEEK	**40**	**41**	**42**	**43**	**44**

Monday Montag Lundi Lunes Lunedì Segunda-feira Maandag 月

•
Ⓓ Tag der Deutschen Einheit
ⓇⓄⓀ National Foundation Day

3

Tuesday Dienstag Mardi Martes Martedì Terça-feira Dinsdag 火

Ⓘⓛ Rosh Hashanah

4

Wednesday Mittwoch Mercredi Miércoles Mercoledì Quarta-feira Woensdag 水

Ⓟ Implantação da República
Ⓘⓛ Rosh Hashanah

5

Thursday Donnerstag Jeudi Jueves Giovedì Quinta-feira Donderdag 木

6

Friday Freitag Vendredi Viernes Venerdì Sexta-feira Vrijdag 金

7

Saturday Samstag Samedi Sábado Sabato Sábado Zaterdag 土

8

Sunday Sonntag Dimanche Domingo Domenica Domingo Zondag 日

9

---

41. WEEK

10.2005

Monday	10	17	24	31	7
Tuesday	11	18	25	1	8
Wednesday	12	19	26	2	9
Thursday	13	20	27	3	10
Friday	14	21	28	4	11
Saturday	15	22	29	5	12
Sunday	16	23	30	6	13
WEEK	41	42	43	44	45

Monday Montag Lundi Lunes Lunedì Segunda-feira Maandag 月

◐

10

(USA) Columbus Day
(CDN) Thanksgiving Day | Action de Grâces
(J) Health-Sports Day

Tuesday Dienstag Mardi Martes Martedì Terça-feira Dinsdag 火

11

Wednesday Mittwoch Mercredi Miércoles Mercoledì Quarta-feira Woensdag 水

(E) Fiesta Nacional

12

Thursday Donnerstag Jeudi Jueves Giovedì Quinta-feira Donderdag 木

(IL) Yom Kippur

13

Friday Freitag Vendredi Viernes Venerdì Sexta-feira Vrijdag 金

14

Saturday Samstag Samedi Sábado Sabato Sábado Zaterdag 土

15

Sunday Sonntag Dimanche Domingo Domenica Domingo Zondag 日

16

La Grenouillère
1869. Oil on canvas, 75 x 100 cm
New York (NY), The Metropolitan Museum of Art

The Path of La Cavée at Pourville
1882. Oil on canvas, 73 x 60 cm
Paris, Collection Durand-Ruel
Photo: Artothek, Weilheim

42. WEEK

10.2005

Monday	17	24	31	7	14
Tuesday	18	25	1	8	15
Wednesday	19	26	2	9	16
Thursday	20	27	3	10	17
Friday	21	28	4	11	18
Saturday	22	29	5	12	19
Sunday	23	30	6	13	20
WEEK	42	43	44	45	46

Monday Montag Lundi Lunes Lunedì Segunda-feira Maandag 月

○

17

Tuesday Dienstag Mardi Martes Martedì Terça-feira Dinsdag 火

(IL) Succoth

18

Wednesday Mittwoch Mercredi Miércoles Mercoledì Quarta-feira Woensdag 水

19

Thursday Donnerstag Jeudi Jueves Giovedì Quinta-feira Donderdag 木

20

Friday Freitag Vendredi Viernes Venerdì Sexta-feira Vrijdag 金

21

Saturday Samstag Samedi Sábado Sabato Sábado Zaterdag 土

22

Sunday Sonntag Dimanche Domingo Domenica Domingo Zondag 日

23

43. ■ WEEK

10.2005

Monday Montag Lundi Lunes Lunedì Segunda-feira Maandag 月

24

Tuesday Dienstag Mardi Martes Martedì Terça-feira Dinsdag 火

◐   (IL) Sh'mini Atzereth

25

Wednesday Mittwoch Mercredi Miércoles Mercoledì Quarta-feira Woensdag 水

                                                                    (A) Nationalfeiertag
                                                                    (IL) Simchat Torah

26

Thursday Donnerstag Jeudi Jueves Giovedì Quinta-feira Donderdag 木

27

Friday Freitag Vendredi Viernes Venerdì Sexta-feira Vrijdag 金

28

Saturday Samstag Samedi Sábado Sabato Sábado Zaterdag 土

29

Sunday Sonntag Dimanche Domingo Domenica Domingo Zondag 日

30

Camille, or The Woman with a Green Dress
1866. Oil on canvas, 231 x 151 cm
Bremen, Kunsthalle Bremen

Following page: **Rouen Cathedral, Sunlight Effect** (detail)
1893. Oil on canvas, 100 x 65 cm
Boston (MA), Museum of Fine Arts

Monday	31	7	14	21	28
Tuesday	1	8	15	22	29
Wednesday	2	9	16	23	30
Thursday	3	10	17	24	1
Friday	4	11	18	25	2
Saturday	5	12	19	26	3
Sunday	6	13	20	27	4
WEEK	**44**	**45**	**46**	**47**	**48**

Monday Montag Lundi Lunes Lunedì Segunda-feira Maandag 月

(IRL) Last Monday in October
(D) Reformationstag (teilweise)

31

Tuesday Dienstag Mardi Martes Martedì Terça-feira Dinsdag 火

(D) Allerheiligen (teilweise)
(F) (A) (E) (I) (P)
Toussaint | Allerheiligen | Todos los
Santos | Ognissanti | Todos os Santos

1

Wednesday Mittwoch Mercredi Miércoles Mercoledì Quarta-feira Woensdag 水

●

2

Thursday Donnerstag Jeudi Jueves Giovedì Quinta-feira Donderdag 木

(J) Culture Day

3

Friday Freitag Vendredi Viernes Venerdì Sexta-feira Vrijdag 金

4

Saturday Samstag Samedi Sábado Sabato Sábado Zaterdag 土

5

Sunday Sonntag Dimanche Domingo Domenica Domingo Zondag 日

6

45. WEEK

11.2005

Monday	7	14	21	28	5
Tuesday	8	15	22	29	6
Wednesday	9	16	23	30	7
Thursday	10	17	24	1	8
Friday	11	18	25	2	9
Saturday	12	19	26	3	10
Sunday	13	20	27	4	11
WEEK	**45**	**46**	**47**	**48**	**49**

Monday Montag Lundi Lunes Lunedì Segunda-feira Maandag 月

7

Tuesday Dienstag Mardi Martes Martedì Terça-feira Dinsdag 火

8

Wednesday Mittwoch Mercredi Miércoles Mercoledì Quarta-feira Woensdag 水

◐

9

Thursday Donnerstag Jeudi Jueves Giovedì Quinta-feira Donderdag 木

10

Friday Freitag Vendredi Viernes Venerdì Sexta-feira Vrijdag 金

(USA) Veterans' Day
(CDN) Remembrance Day | Jour du Souvenir
(F) Armistice 1918

11

Saturday Samstag Samedi Sábado Sabato Sábado Zaterdag 土

12

Sunday Sonntag Dimanche Domingo Domenica Domingo Zondag 日

13

Camille Monet on her Deathbed
1879. Oil on canvas, 90 x 68 cm
Paris, Musée d'Orsay

Water-Lilies
1914–1917, Oil on canvas, 200 x 200 cm
Paris, Musée Marmottan

46. WEEK

11.2005

Monday	14	21	28	5	12
Tuesday	15	22	29	6	13
Wednesday	16	23	30	7	14
Thursday	17	24	1	8	15
Friday	18	25	2	9	16
Saturday	19	26	3	10	17
Sunday	20	27	4	11	18
WEEK	**46**	**47**	**48**	**49**	**50**

Monday Montag Lundi Lunes Lunedì Segunda-feira Maandag 月

14

Tuesday Dienstag Mardi Martes Martedì Terça-feira Dinsdag 火

15

Wednesday Mittwoch Mercredi Miércoles Mercoledì Quarta-feira Woensdag 水

Ⓓ Buß- und Bettag (teilweise)

16

Thursday Donnerstag Jeudi Jueves Giovedì Quinta-feira Donderdag 木

17

Friday Freitag Vendredi Viernes Venerdì Sexta-feira Vrijdag 金

18

Saturday Samstag Samedi Sábado Sabato Sábado Zaterdag 土

19

Sunday Sonntag Dimanche Domingo Domenica Domingo Zondag 日

20

47. WEEK

11.2005

Monday	21	28	5	12	19
Tuesday	22	29	6	13	20
Wednesday	23	30	7	14	21
Thursday	24	1	8	15	22
Friday	25	2	9	16	23
Saturday	26	3	10	17	24
Sunday	27	4	11	18	25
WEEK	47	48	49	50	51

Monday Montag Lundi Lunes Lunedì Segunda-feira Maandag 月

21

Tuesday Dienstag Mardi Martes Martedì Terça-feira Dinsdag 火

22

Wednesday Mittwoch Mercredi Miércoles Mercoledì Quarta-feira Woensdag 水

◗   Ⓙ Labor-Thanksgiving Day

23

Thursday Donnerstag Jeudi Jueves Giovedì Quinta-feira Donderdag 木

USA Thanksgiving Day

24

Friday Freitag Vendredi Viernes Venerdì Sexta-feira Vrijdag 金

25

Saturday Samstag Samedi Sábado Sabato Sábado Zaterdag 土

26

Sunday Sonntag Dimanche Domingo Domenica Domingo Zondag 日

27

Turkeys
1876. Oil on canvas, 172 x 175 cm
Paris, Musée d'Orsay

Following page:
Asters
1880. Oil on canvas, 83 x 68.5 cm
New York, Christie's
Photo: Artothek, Weilheim / Christie's Images

48. WEEK

11|12.2005

Monday	28	5	12	19	26
Tuesday	29	6	13	20	27
Wednesday	30	7	14	21	28
Thursday	1	8	15	22	29
Friday	2	9	16	23	30
Saturday	3	10	17	24	31
Sunday	4	11	18	25	1
WEEK	**48**	**49**	**50**	**51**	**52**

Monday Montag Lundi Lunes Lunedì Segunda-feira Maandag 月

28

Tuesday Dienstag Mardi Martes Martedì Terça-feira Dinsdag 火

29

Wednesday Mittwoch Mercredi Miércoles Mercoledì Quarta-feira Woensdag 水

30

Thursday Donnerstag Jeudi Jueves Giovedì Quinta-feira Donderdag 木

(P) Dia da Restauração

1

Friday Freitag Vendredi Viernes Venerdì Sexta-feira Vrijdag 金

2

Saturday Samstag Samedi Sábado Sabato Sábado Zaterdag 土

3

Sunday Sonntag Dimanche Domingo Domenica Domingo Zondag 日

4

49. ∎ WEEK

12.2005

Monday	5	12	19	26	2
Tuesday	6	13	20	27	3
Wednesday	7	14	21	28	4
Thursday	8	15	22	29	5
Friday	9	16	23	30	6
Saturday	10	17	24	31	7
Sunday	11	18	25	1	8
WEEK	49	50	51	52	1

Monday Montag Lundi Lunes Lunedì Segunda-feira Maandag 月

5

Tuesday Dienstag Mardi Martes Martedì Terça-feira Dinsdag 火

(E) Día de la Constitución

6

Wednesday Mittwoch Mercredi Miércoles Mercoledì Quarta-feira Woensdag 水

7

Thursday Donnerstag Jeudi Jueves Giovedì Quinta-feira Donderdag 木

◐

(A) (E) (I) (P)
Mariä Empfängnis | Inmaculada
Concepción | Immacolata Concezione
Imaculada Conceição

8

Friday Freitag Vendredi Viernes Venerdì Sexta-feira Vrijdag 金

9

Saturday Samstag Samedi Sábado Sabato Sábado Zaterdag 土

10

Sunday Sonntag Dimanche Domingo Domenica Domingo Zondag 日

11

The Boulevard des Capucines
1873. Oil on canvas, 80 x 60 cm
Kansas City (MO), The Nelson-Atkins Museum of Art

Camille Monet in Japanese Costume
1875. Oil on canvas, 231.5 x 142 cm
Boston (MA), Museum of Fine Arts

50. ■ WEEK

12.2005

Monday	12	19	26	2	9
Tuesday	13	20	27	3	10
Wednesday	14	21	28	4	11
Thursday	15	22	29	5	12
Friday	16	23	30	6	13
Saturday	17	24	31	7	14
Sunday	18	25	1	8	15
WEEK	**50**	**51**	**52**	**1**	**2**

Monday Montag Lundi Lunes Lunedì Segunda-feira Maandag 月

12

Tuesday Dienstag Mardi Martes Martedì Terça-feira Dinsdag 火

13

Wednesday Mittwoch Mercredi Miércoles Mercoledì Quarta-feira Woensdag 水

14

Thursday Donnerstag Jeudi Jueves Giovedì Quinta-feira Donderdag 木
○

15

Friday Freitag Vendredi Viernes Venerdì Sexta-feira Vrijdag 金

16

Saturday Samstag Samedi Sábado Sabato Sábado Zaterdag 土

17

Sunday Sonntag Dimanche Domingo Domenica Domingo Zondag 日

18

51. WEEK

12.2005

Monday	19	26	2	9	16
Tuesday	20	27	3	10	17
Wednesday	21	28	4	11	18
Thursday	22	29	5	12	19
Friday	23	30	6	13	20
Saturday	24	31	7	14	21
Sunday	25	1	8	15	22
WEEK	51	52	1	2	3

Monday Montag Lundi Lunes Lunedì Segunda-feira Maandag 月

19

Tuesday Dienstag Mardi Martes Martedì Terça-feira Dinsdag 火

20

Wednesday Mittwoch Mercredi Miércoles Mercoledì Quarta-feira Woensdag 水

21

Thursday Donnerstag Jeudi Jueves Giovedì Quinta-feira Donderdag 木

22

Friday Freitag Vendredi Viernes Venerdì Sexta-feira Vrijdag 金

◗   (J) Emperor's Birthday

23

Saturday Samstag Samedi Sábado Sabato Sábado Zaterdag 土

24

Sunday Sonntag Dimanche Domingo Domenica Domingo Zondag 日

(USA) (UK) (IRL) (ROK) (CDN) (F) (D) (A) (CH)
(NL) (E) (I) (P)
Christmas Day | Noël | 1. Weihnachtstag
Weihnachten | 1e Kerstdag | Natividad
del Señor | Natale | Dia de Natal

25

Still Life with Pheasant
c. 1861. Oil on canvas, 76 x 62.5 cm
Rouen, Musée des Beaux-Arts et de la Céramique
Photo: Artothek, Weilheim

Previous page: **Gondolas in Venice**
1908. Oil on canvas, 81 x 55 cm
Nantes, Musée des Beaux-Arts de Nantes
Photo: Giraudon / Bridgeman Art Library

Last page: **Undergrowth in Argenteuil**
1875. Oil on canvas, 80 x 60 cm
New York, Christie's
Photo: Artothek, Weilheim / Christie's Images

52. WEEK 12.2005 | 01.2006

Monday	26	2	9	16	23
Tuesday	27	3	10	17	24
Wednesday	28	4	11	18	25
Thursday	29	5	12	19	26
Friday	30	6	13	20	27
Saturday	31	7	14	21	28
Sunday	1	8	15	22	29
WEEK	**52**	**1**	**2**	**3**	**4**

Monday Montag Lundi Lunes Lunedì Segunda-feira Maandag 月

(UK) (IRL) (CDN) (D) (A) (CH) (NL) (I)
Boxing Day | Saint Stephen's Day |
Lendemain de Noël | 2. Weihnachtstag |
Stefanstag | S. Etienne | 2e Kerstdag |
S. Stefano
(IL) Hanukkah

26

Tuesday Dienstag Mardi Martes Martedì Terça-feira Dinsdag 火

(UK) Public Holiday

27

Wednesday Mittwoch Mercredi Miércoles Mercoledì Quarta-feira Woensdag 水

28

Thursday Donnerstag Jeudi Jueves Giovedì Quinta-feira Donderdag 木

29

Friday Freitag Vendredi Viernes Venerdì Sexta-feira Vrijdag 金

30

Saturday Samstag Samedi Sábado Sabato Sábado Zaterdag 土

31

Sunday Sonntag Dimanche Domingo Domenica Domingo Zondag 日

New Year's Day | Jour de l'An | Neujahr |
Nieuwjaarsdag | Nieuwjaar | Nouvel An |
Capodanno

1

PUBLIC HOLIDAYS 2005

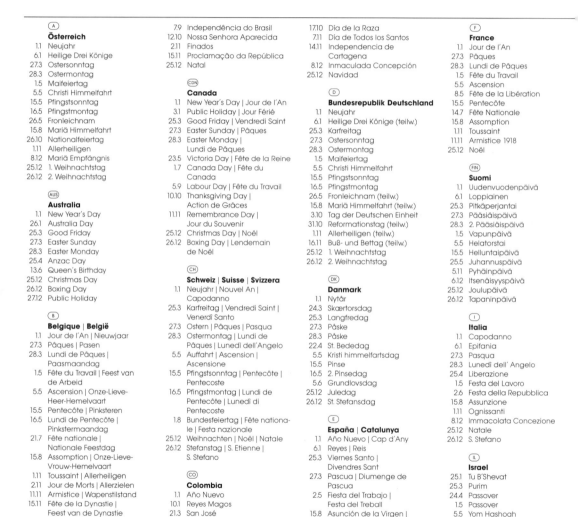

(A) Österreich
1.1 Neujahr
6.1 Heilige Drei Könige
27.3 Ostersonntag
28.3 Ostermontag
1.5 Maifeiertag
5.5 Christi Himmelfahrt
15.5 Pfingstsonntag
16.5 Pfingstmontag
26.5 Fronleichnam
15.8 Mariä Himmelfahrt
26.10 Nationalfeiertag
1.11 Allerheiligen
8.12 Mariä Empfängnis
25.12 1. Weihnachtstag
26.12 2. Weihnachtstag

(AUS) Australia
1.1 New Year's Day
26.1 Australia Day
25.3 Good Friday
27.3 Easter Sunday
28.3 Easter Monday
25.4 Anzac Day
13.6 Queen's Birthday
25.12 Christmas Day
26.12 Boxing Day
27.12 Public Holiday

(B) Belgique | België
1.1 Jour de l'An | Nieuwjaar
27.3 Pâques | Pasen
28.3 Lundi de Pâques |
Paasmaandag
1.5 Fête du Travail | Feest van
de Arbeid
5.5 Ascension | Onze-Lieve-
Heer-Hemelvaart
15.5 Pentecôte | Pinksteren
16.5 Lundi de Pentecôte |
Pinkstermaandag
21.7 Fête nationale |
Nationale Feestdag
15.8 Assomption | Onze-Lieve-
Vrouw-Hemelvaart
1.11 Toussaint | Allerheiligen
2.11 Jour de Morts | Allerzielen
11.11 Armistice | Wapenstilstand
15.11 Fête de la Dynastie |
Feest van de Dynastie
25.12 Noël | Kerstmis

(BR) Brasil
1.1 Ano Novo
8.2 Carnaval
25.3 Sexta-feira da Paixão
27.3 Páscoa
21.4 Tiradentes
1.5 Dia do Trabalho
26.5 Corpus Christi

7.9 Independência do Brasil
12.10 Nossa Senhora Aparecida
2.11 Finados
15.11 Proclamação da República
25.12 Natal

(CDN) Canada
1.1 New Year's Day | Jour de l'An
3.1 Public Holiday | Jour Férié
25.3 Good Friday | Vendredi Saint
27.3 Easter Sunday | Pâques
28.3 Easter Monday |
Lundi de Pâques
23.5 Victoria Day | Fête de la Reine
1.7 Canada Day | Fête du
Canada
5.9 Labour Day | Fête du Travail
10.10 Thanksgiving Day |
Action de Grâces
11.11 Remembrance Day |
Jour du Souvenir
25.12 Christmas Day | Noël
26.12 Boxing Day | Lendemain
de Noël

(CH) Schweiz | Suisse | Svizzera
1.1 Neujahr | Nouvel An |
Capodanno
25.3 Karfreitag | Vendredi Saint |
Venerdì Santo
27.3 Ostern | Pâques | Pasqua
28.3 Ostermontag | Lundi de
Pâques | Lunedì dell'Angelo
5.5 Auffahrt | Ascension |
Ascensione
15.5 Pfingstsonntag | Pentecôte |
Pentecoste
16.5 Pfingstmontag | Lundi de
Pentecôte | Lunedì di
Pentecoste
1.8 Bundesfeiertag | Fête nationa-
le | Festa nazionale
25.12 Weihnachten | Noël | Natale
26.12 Stefanstag | S. Etienne |
S. Stefano

(CO) Colombia
1.1 Año Nuevo
10.1 Reyes Magos
21.3 San José
24.3 Jueves Santo
25.3 Viernes Santo
27.3 Pascua
1.5 Día del Trabajo
9.5 Ascensión del Señor
30.5 Corpus Christi
6.6 Sagrado Corazón
4.7 San Pedro y San Pablo
20.7 Independencia Nacional
7.8 Batalla de Boyacá
15.8 Asunción de la Virgen

17.10 Día de la Raza
7.11 Día de Todos los Santos
14.11 Independencia de
Cartagena
8.12 Inmaculada Concepción
25.12 Navidad

(D) Bundesrepublik Deutschland
1.1 Neujahr
6.1 Heilige Drei Könige (teilw.)
25.3 Karfreitag
27.3 Ostersonntag
28.3 Ostermontag
1.5 Maifeiertag
5.5 Christi Himmelfahrt
15.5 Pfingstsonntag
16.5 Pfingstmontag
26.5 Fronleichnam (teilw.)
15.8 Mariä Himmelfahrt (teilw.)
3.10 Tag der Deutschen Einheit
31.10 Reformationstag (teilw.)
1.11 Allerheiligen (teilw.)
16.11 Buß- und Bettag (teilw.)
25.12 1. Weihnachtstag
26.12 2. Weihnachtstag

(DK) Danmark
1.1 Nytår
24.3 Skærtorsdag
25.3 Langfredag
27.3 Påske
28.3 Påske
22.4 St. Bededag
5.5 Kristi himmelfartsdag
15.5 Pinse
16.5 2. Pinsedag
5.6 Grundlovsdag
25.12 Juledag
26.12 St. Stefansdag

(E) España | Catalunya
1.1 Año Nuevo | Cap d'Any
6.1 Reyes | Reis
25.3 Viernes Santo |
Divendres Sant
27.3 Pascua | Diumenge de
Pascua
2.5 Fiesta del Trabajo |
Festa del Treball
15.8 Asunción de la Virgen |
L'Assumpció
12.10 Fiesta Nacional | Festa
Nacional d'Espanya
1.11 Todos los Santos | Tots Sants
6.12 Día de la Constitución |
Dia de la Constitució
8.12 Inmaculada Concepción |
La Immaculada
25.12 Natividad del Señor | Nadal

(F) France
1.1 Jour de l'An
27.3 Pâques
28.3 Lundi de Pâques
1.5 Fête du Travail
5.5 Ascension
8.5 Fête de la Libération
15.5 Pentecôte
14.7 Fête Nationale
15.8 Assomption
1.11 Toussaint
11.11 Armistice 1918
25.12 Noël

(FIN) Suomi
1.1 Uudenvuodenpäivä
6.1 Loppiainen
25.3 Pitkäperjantai
27.3 Pääsiäispäivä
28.3 2. Pääsiäispäivä
1.5 Vapunpäivä
5.5 Helatorstai
15.5 Helluntaipäivä
25.5 Juhannuspäivä
5.11 Pyhäinpäivä
6.12 Itsenäisyyspäivä
25.12 Joulupäivä
26.12 Tapaninpäivä

(I) Italia
1.1 Capodanno
6.1 Epifania
27.3 Pasqua
28.3 Lunedì dell' Angelo
25.4 Liberazione
1.5 Festa del Lavoro
2.6 Festa della Repubblica
15.8 Assunzione
1.11 Ognissanti
8.12 Immacolata Concezione
25.12 Natale
26.12 S. Stefano

(IL) Israel
25.1 Tu B'Shevat
25.3 Purim
24.4 Passover
1.5 Passover
5.5 Yom Hashoah
12.5 Yom Haatzmaut
13.6 Shavuot
14.8 Tisha B'Av
4.10 Rosh Hashanah
5.10 Rosh Hashanah
13.10 Yom Kippur
18.10 Succoth
25.10 Sh'mini Atzereth
26.10 Simchat Torah
26.12 Hanukkah

PUBLIC HOLIDAYS 2005

(IRL) Ireland
1.1 New Year's Day
17.3 Saint Patrick's Day
27.3 Easter Sunday
28.3 Easter Monday
2.5 First Monday in May
6.6 First Monday in June
1.8 First Monday in August
31.10 Last Monday in October
25.12 Christmas Day
26.12 Saint Stephen's Day

(J) Japan
1.1 New Year's Day
10.1 Coming-of-Age Day
11.2 Commemoration of the Founding of the Nation
20.3 Vernal Equinox Day
21.3 Public Holiday
29.4 Greenery Day
3.5 Constitution Day
4.5 Public Holiday
5.5 Children's Day
18.7 Marine Day
19.9 Respect-for-the-Aged Day
23.9 Autumn Equinox Day
10.10 Health-Sports Day
3.11 Culture Day
23.11 Labor-Thanksgiving Day
23.12 Emperor's Birthday

(L) Luxembourg
1.1 Jour de l'An
27.3 Pâques
28.3 Lundi de Pâques
1.5 Fête du Travail
5.5 Ascension
15.5 Pentecôte
16.5 Lundi de Pentecôte
23.6 Fête Nationale
15.8 Assomption
1.11 Toussaint
25.12 Noël
26.12 Lendemain de Noël

(MEX) México
1.1 Año Nuevo
5.2 Aniversario de la Constitución
21.3 Natalicio de Benito Juárez
24.3 Jueves Santo
25.3 Viernes Santo
27.3 Pascua
1.5 Día del Trabajo
1.9 Informe presidencial
16.9 Día de la Independencia
20.11 Aniversario de la Revolución Mexicana
25.12 Navidad

(N) Norge
1.1 Nyttårsdag
20.3 Palmesøndag
24.3 Skjærtorsdag
25.3 Langfredag
27.3 1. påskedag
28.3 2. påskedag
1.5 Offentlig høytidsdag
17.5 Grunnlovsdag
5.5 Kristi himmelfartsdag
15.5 1. pinsedag
16.5 2. pinsedag
25.12 1. juledag
26.12 2. juledag

(NL) Nederland
1.1 Nieuwjaarsdag
27.3 1e Paasdag
28.3 2e Paasdag
30.4 Koninginnedag
5.5 Hemelvaartsdag
15.5 1e Pinksterdag
16.5 2e Pinksterdag
25.12 1e Kerstdag
26.12 2e Kerstdag

(NZ) New Zealand
1.1 New Year's Day
2.1 Day after New Year's Day
6.2 Waitangi Day
25.3 Good Friday
27.3 Easter Sunday
28.3 Easter Monday
25.4 Anzac Day
6.6 Queen's Birthday
24.10 Labour Day
25.12 Christmas Day
26.12 Boxing Day
27.12 Public Holiday

(P) Portugal
1.1 Ano Novo
25.3 Sexta-feira Santa
27.3 Domingo de Páscoa
25.4 Dia da Liberdade
1.5 Dia do Trabalhador
26.5 Corpo de Deus
10.6 Dia Nacional
15.8 Assunção de Nossa Senhora
5.10 Implantação da República
1.11 Todos os Santos
1.12 Dia da Restauração
8.12 Imaculada Conceição
25.12 Dia de Natal

(RA) Argentina
1.1 Año Nuevo
24.3 Jueves Santo
25.3 Viernes Santo
27.3 Pascua
4.4 Recuperación de las Islas Malvinas
1.5 Día del Trabajador
25.5 Fundación del Primer Gobierno Nacional
20.6 Día de la Bandera
9.7 Día de la Independencia
17.8 Muerte del General San Martín
12.10 Descubrimiento de América
8.12 Inmaculada Concepción de la Virgen María
25.12 Navidad

(RCH) Chile
1.1 Año Nuevo
25.3 Viernes Santo
27.3 Pascua
1.5 Día del Trabajo
21.5 Combate Naval de Iquique
23.5 Corpus Christi
15.8 Asunción de la Virgen
18.9 Fiestas Patrias
19.9 Día del Ejército
12.10 Día de la Hispanidad
1.11 Todos los Santos
8.12 Inmaculada Concepción
25.12 Navidad

(ROK) Korea
1.1 New Year's Day
1.3 Independence Movement Day
5.4 Arbor Day
5.5 Children's Day
15.5 Buddha's Birthday
6.6 Memorial Day
17.7 Constitution Day
15.8 Independence Day
18.9 Chuseok
3.10 National Foundation Day
25.12 Christmas Day

(S) Sverige
1.1 Nyårsdagen
6.1 Trettondedag jul
25.3 Långfredagen
27.3 Påskdagen
28.3 Annandag påsk
1.5 Första maj
5.5 Kristi himmelsfärds dag
15.5 Pingstdagen
16.5 Annandag pingst
25.6 Midsommardagen
5.11 Alla helgons dag
25.12 Juldagen
26.12 Annandag jul

(UK) United Kingdom
1.1 New Year's Day
3.1 Public Holiday
4.1 Public Holiday (Scotland only)
17.3 Saint Patrick's Day (Northern Ireland only)
25.3 Good Friday
27.3 Easter Sunday
28.3 Easter Monday (except Scotland)
2.5 May Bank Holiday
30.5 Spring Bank Holiday
12.7 Battle of the Boyne Day (Northern Ireland only)
1.8 Summer Bank Holiday (Scotland only)
29.8 Summer Bank Holiday (except Scotland)
25.12 Christmas Day
26.12 Boxing Day
27.12 Public Holiday

(USA) United States
1.1 New Year's Day
17.1 Martin Luther King Day
21.2 President's Day
27.3 Easter Sunday
30.5 Memorial Day
4.7 Independence Day
5.9 Labor Day
10.10 Columbus Day
11.11 Veterans' Day
24.11 Thanksgiving Day
25.12 Christmas Day

(ZA) South Africa
1.1 New Year's Day
21.3 Human Rights Day
25.3 Good Friday
27.3 Easter Sunday
28.3 Family Day
27.4 Freedom Day
1.5 Workers' Day
2.5 Public Holiday
16.6 Youth Day
9.8 National Women's Day
24.9 Heritage Day
16.12 Day of Reconciliation
25.12 Christmas Day
26.12 Day of Goodwill

Some international holidays may be subject to change.

YEAR PLANNER

JANUARY	FEBRUARY	MARCH	APRIL
1 Su	1 We	1 We	1 Sa
WEEK 1	2 Th	2 Th	2 Su
2 Mo	3 Fr	3 Fr	**WEEK 14**
3 Tu	4 Sa	4 Sa	3 Mo
4 We	5 Su ◐	5 Su	4 Tu
5 Th	**WEEK 6**	**WEEK 10**	5 We ◐
6 Fr ◐	6 Mo ◐	6 Mo ◐	6 Th
7 Sa	7 Tu	7 Tu	7 Fr
8 Su	8 We	8 We	8 Sa
WEEK 2	9 Th	9 Th	9 Su
9 Mo	10 Fr	10 Fr	**WEEK 15**
10 Tu	11 Sa	11 Sa	10 Mo
11 We	12 Su	12 Su	11 Tu
12 Th	**WEEK 7**	**WEEK 11**	12 We
13 Fr	13 Mo ○	13 Mo	13 Th ○
14 Sa ○	14 Tu	14 Tu ○	14 Fr
15 Su	15 We	15 We	15 Sa
WEEK 3	16 Th	16 Th	16 Su
16 Mo	17 Fr	17 Fr	**WEEK 16**
17 Tu	18 Sa	18 Sa	17 Mo
18 We	19 Su	19 Su	18 Tu
19 Th	**WEEK 8**	**WEEK 12**	19 We
20 Fr	20 Mo	20 Mo	20 Th
21 Sa	21 Tu ◑	21 Tu	21 Fr ◑
22 Su ◑	22 We	22 We ◑	22 Sa
WEEK 4	23 Th ○	23 Th	23 Su
23 Mo	24 Fr	24 Fr	**WEEK 17**
24 Tu	25 Sa	25 Sa	24 Mo
25 We	26 Su	26 Su	25 Tu
26 Th	**WEEK 9**	**WEEK 13**	26 We
27 Fr	27 Mo	27 Mo	27 Th ●
28 Sa	28 Tu ●	28 Tu	28 Fr
29 Su ●		29 We ●	29 Sa
WEEK 5		30 Th	30 Su
30 Mo		31 Fr	
31 Tu			

05–08.2006

MAY	JUNE	JULY	AUGUST
WEEK 18	1 Th	1 Sa	1 Tu
1 Mo	2 Fr	2 Su	2 We ◑
2 Tu	3 Sa ◑	**WEEK 27**	3 Th
3 We	4 Su	3 Mo ◑	4 Fr
4 Th	**WEEK 23**	4 Tu	5 Sa
5 Fr ◑	5 Mo	5 We	6 Su
6 Sa	6 Tu	6 Th	**WEEK 32**
7 Su	7 We	7 Fr	7 Mo
WEEK 19	8 Th	8 Sa	8 Tu
8 Mo	9 Fr	9 Su	9 We ○
9 Tu	10 Sa	**WEEK 28**	10 Th
10 We	11 Su ○	10 Mo	11 Fr
11 Th	**WEEK 24**	11 Tu ○	12 Sa
12 Fr	12 Mo	12 We	13 Su
13 Sa ○	13 Tu	13 Th	**WEEK 33**
14 Su	14 We	14 Fr	14 Mo
WEEK 20	15 Th	15 Sa	15 Tu
15 Mo	16 Fr	16 Su	16 We ◐
16 Tu	17 Sa	**WEEK 29**	17 Th
17 We	18 Su ◐	17 Mo ◐	18 Fr
18 Th	**WEEK 25**	18 Tu	19 Sa
19 Fr	19 Mo	19 We	20 Su
20 Sa ◐	20 Tu	20 Th	**WEEK 34**
21 Su	21 We	21 Fr	21 Mo
WEEK 21	22 Th	22 Sa	22 Tu
22 Mo	23 Fr	23 Su	23 We ●
23 Tu	24 Sa	**WEEK 30**	24 Th
24 We	25 Su ●	24 Mo	25 Fr
25 Th	**WEEK 26**	25 Tu ●	26 Sa
26 Fr	26 Mo	26 We	27 Su
27 Sa ●	27 Tu	27 Th	**WEEK 35**
28 Su	28 We	28 Fr	28 Mo
WEEK 22	29 Th	29 Sa	29 Tu
29 Mo	30 Fr	30 Su	30 We
30 Tu		**WEEK 31**	31 Th ◑
31 We		31 Mo	

SEPTEMBER	OCTOBER	NOVEMBER	DECEMBER
1 Fr	1 Su	1 We	1 Fr
2 Sa	**WEEK 40**	2 Th	2 Sa
3 Su	2 Mo	3 Fr	3 Su
WEEK 36	3 Tu	4 Sa	**WEEK 49**
4 Mo	4 We	5 Su ○	4 Mo
5 Tu	5 Th	**WEEK 45**	5 Tu ○
6 We	6 Fr	6 Mo	6 We
7 Th ○	7 Sa ○	7 Tu	7 Th
8 Fr	8 Su	8 We	8 Fr
9 Sa	**WEEK 41**	9 Th	9 Sa
10 Su	9 Mo	10 Fr	10 Su
WEEK 37	10 Tu	11 Sa	**WEEK 50**
11 Mo	11 We	12 Su ☽	11 Mo
12 Tu	12 Th	**WEEK 46**	12 Tu ☽
13 We	13 Fr	13 Mo	13 We
14 Th ☽	14 Sa ☽	14 Tu	14 Th
15 Fr	15 Su	15 We	15 Fr
16 Sa	**WEEK 42**	16 Th	16 Sa
17 Su	16 Mo	17 Fr	17 Su
WEEK 38	17 Tu	18 Sa	**WEEK 51**
18 Mo	18 We	19 Su	18 Mo
19 Tu	19 Th	**WEEK 47**	19 Tu
20 We	20 Fr	20 Mo ●	20 We ●
21 Th	21 Sa	21 Tu	21 Th
22 Fr ●	22 Su ●	22 We	22 Fr
23 Sa	**WEEK 43**	23 Th	23 Sa
24 Su	23 Mo	24 Fr	24 Su
WEEK 39	24 Tu	25 Sa	**WEEK 52**
25 Mo	25 We	26 Su	25 Mo
26 Tu	26 Th	**WEEK 48**	26 Tu
27 We	27 Fr	27 Mo	27 We ☾
28 Th	28 Sa	28 Tu ☾	28 Th
29 Fr	29 Su ☾	29 We	29 Fr
30 Sa ☾	**WEEK 44**	30 Th	30 Sa
	30 Mo		31 Su
	31 Tu